An insect has six legs.

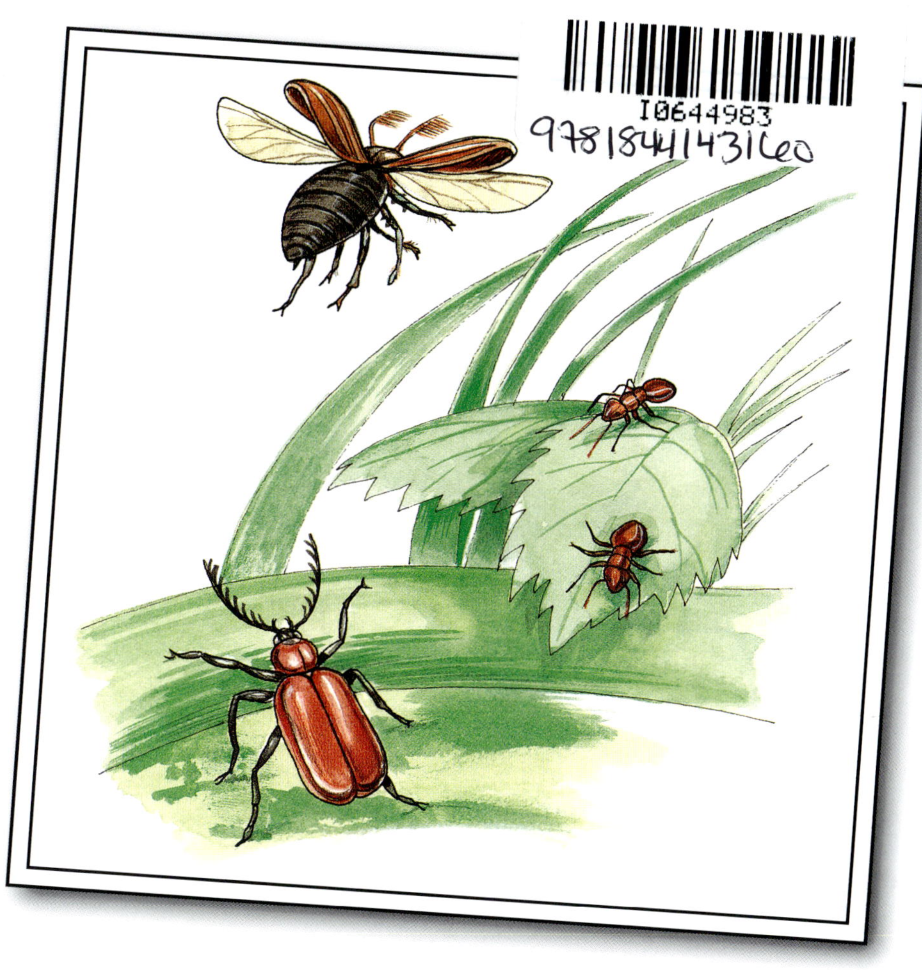

It has a hard skin.

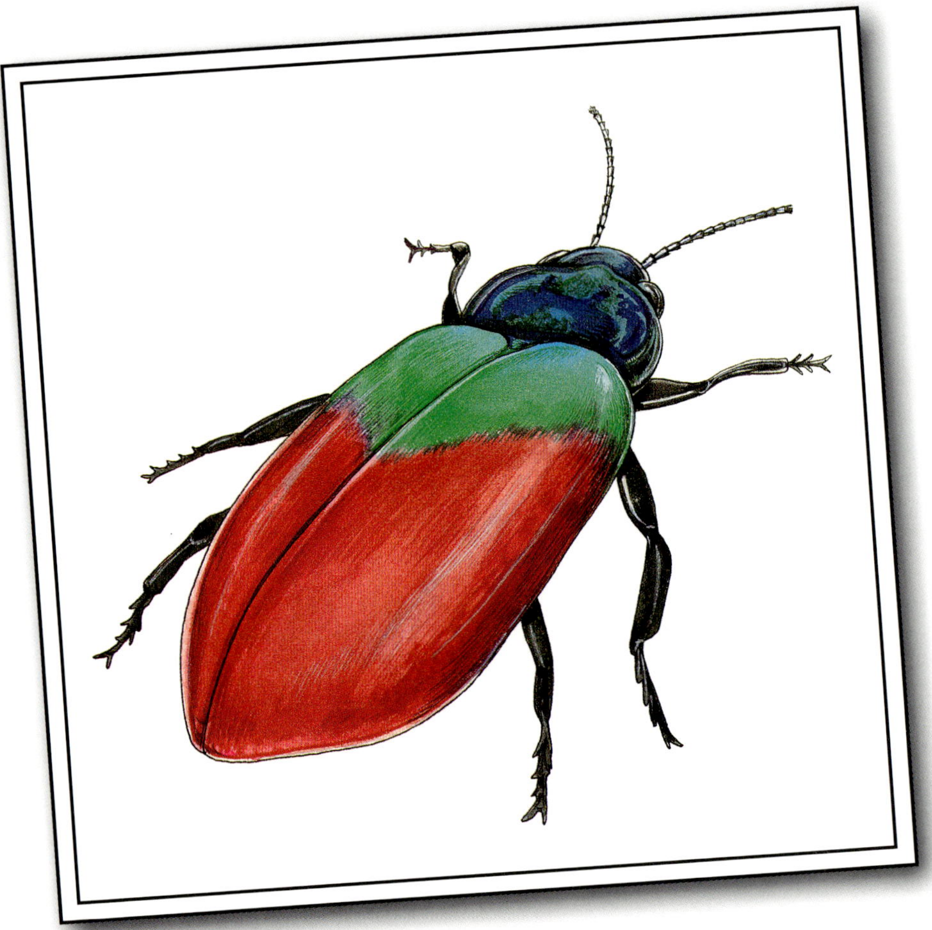

Insects can shed this skin to get bigger.

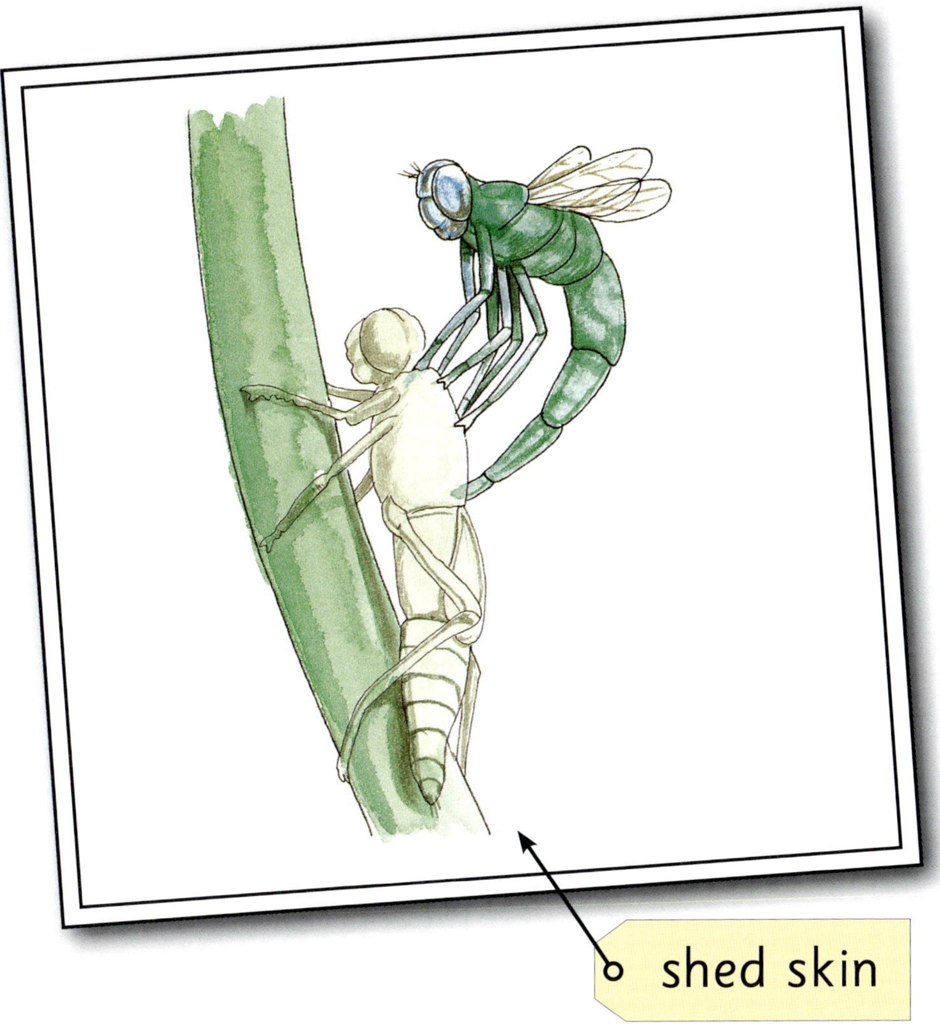

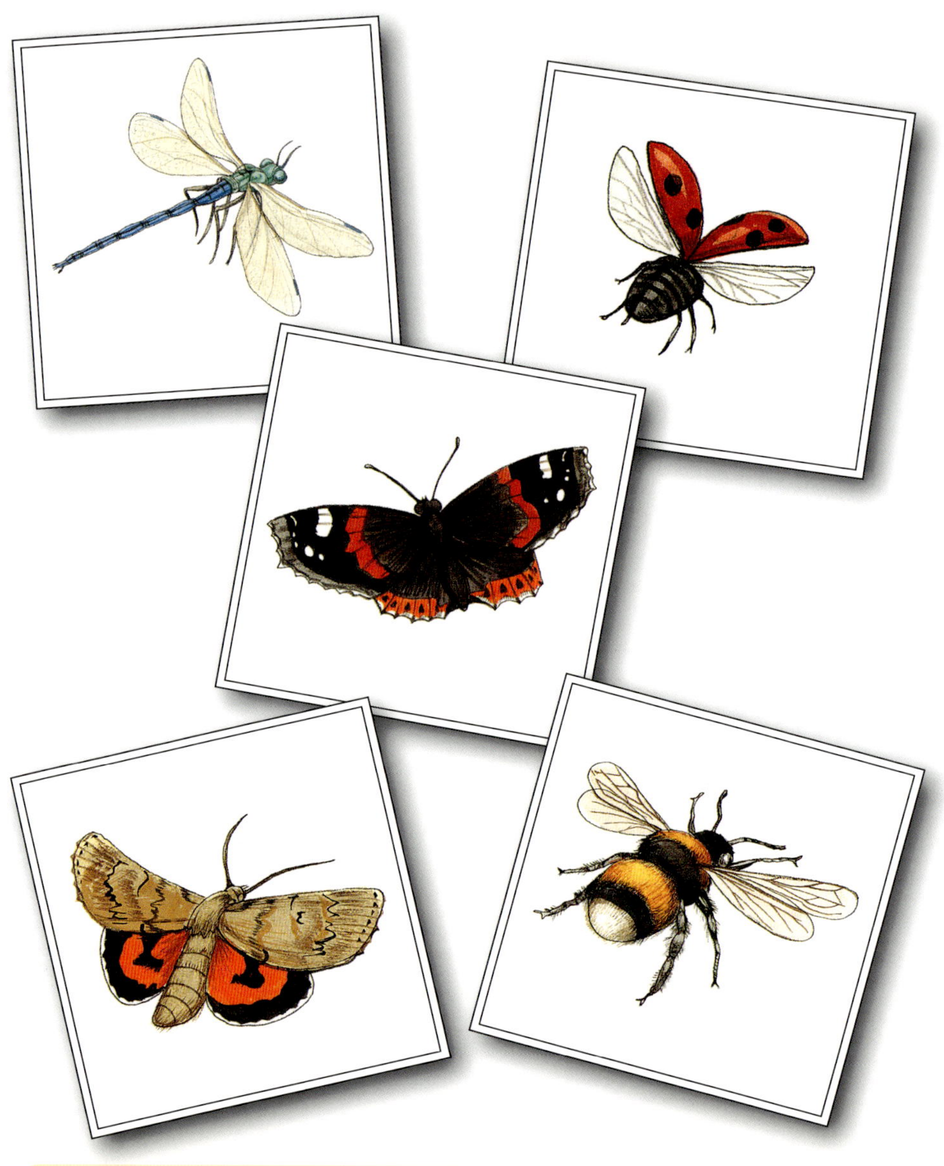

Lots of insects have wings.

Insects hatch from eggs...

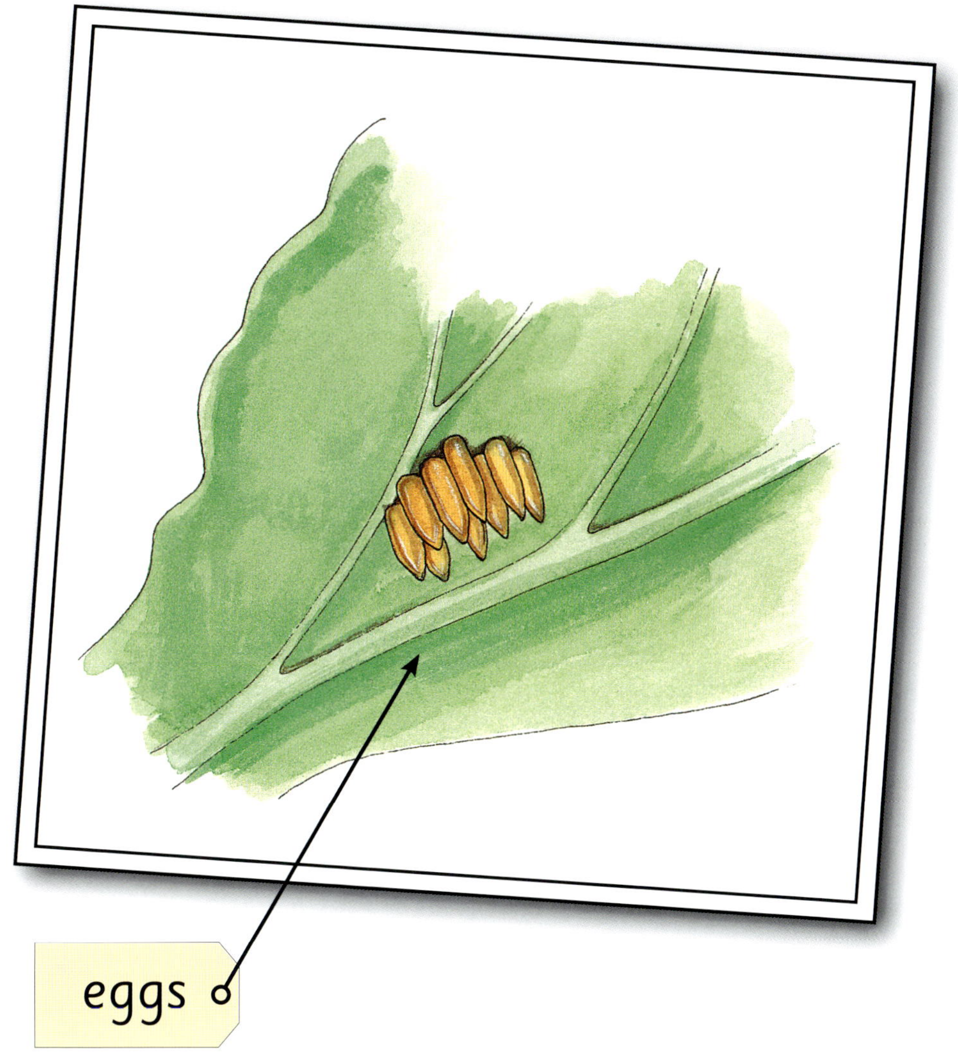

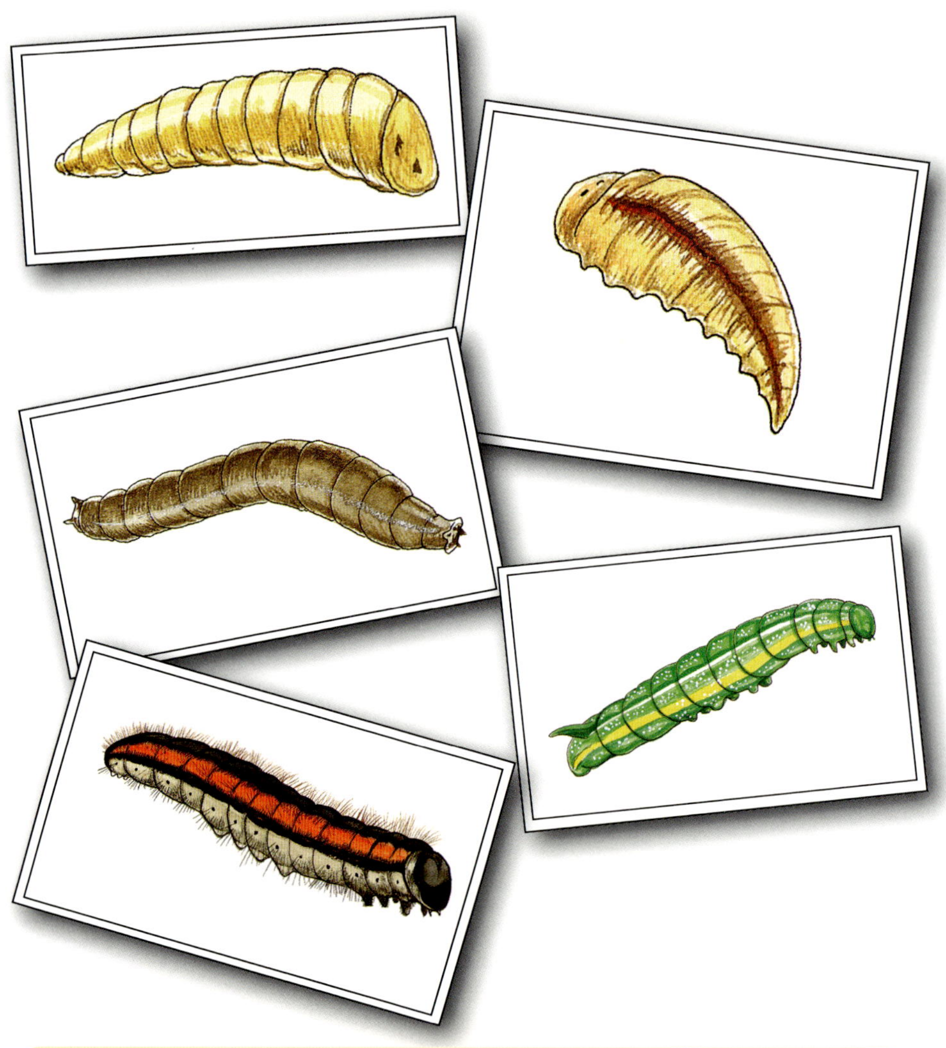

...and start as grubs, maggots, or caterpillars.

Born as caterpillars...

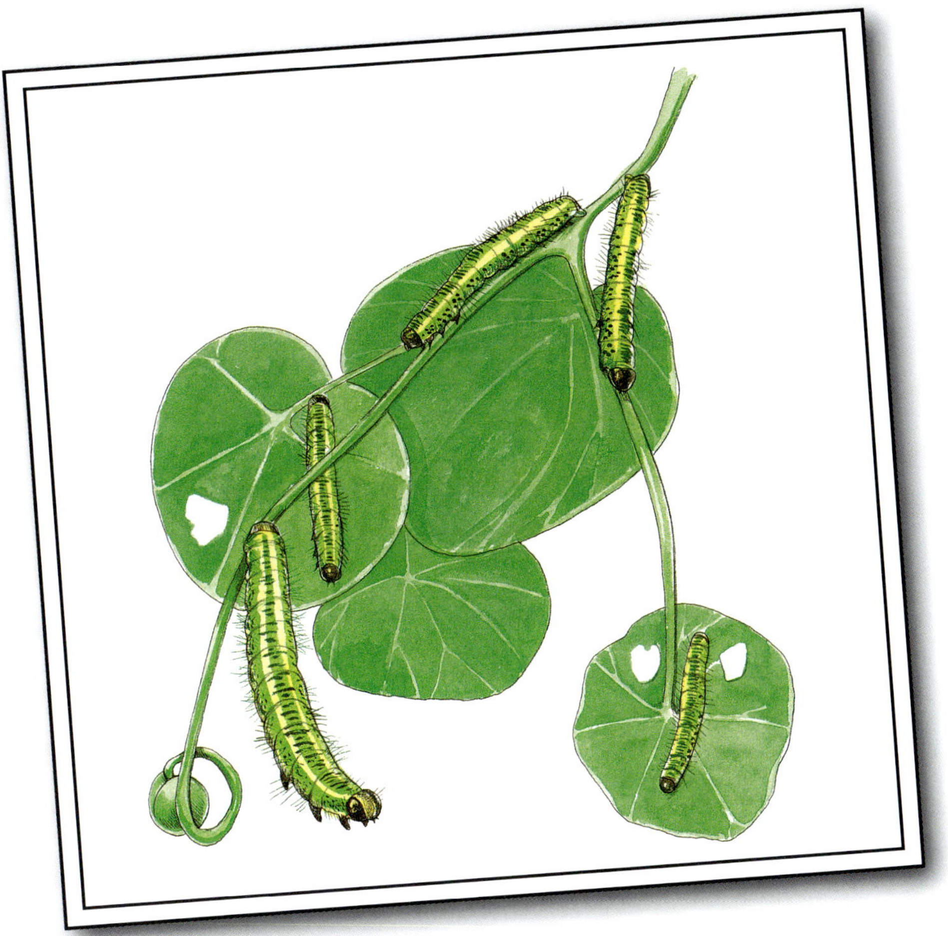

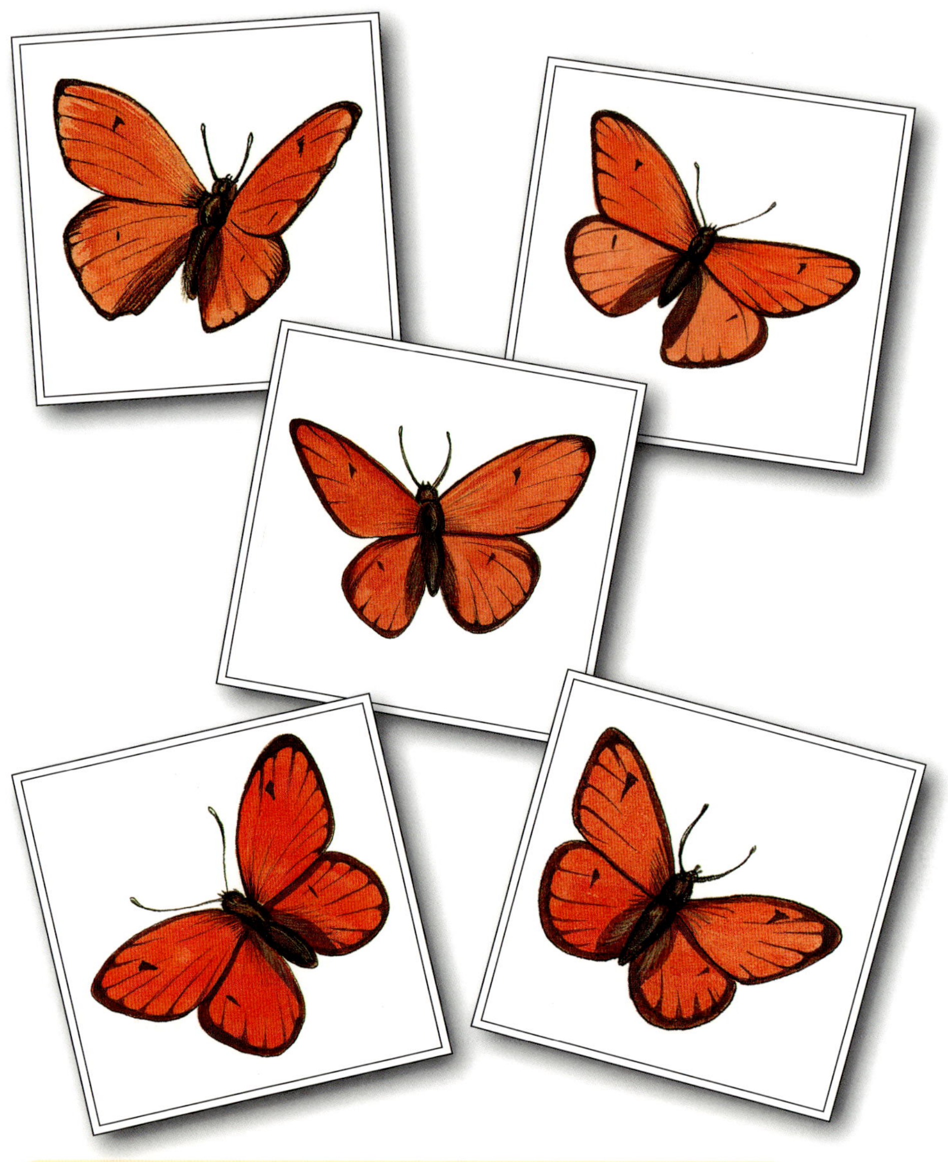

...end as butterflies!